DEBRIS

Dennis Kelly

DEBRIS

OBERON BOOKS

LONDON

First published in this version in 2004 by Oberon Books Ltd.
(incorporating Absolute Classics)
521 Caledonian Road, London N7 9RH
Tel: 020 7607 3637 / Fax: 020 7607 3629

e-mail: oberon.books@btinternet.com
www.oberonbooks.com

A catalogue record for this book is available from the
British Library.

ISBN: 1 84002 433 X

Printed in Great Britain by Antony Rowe Ltd, Chippenham.

Characters

MICHAEL

MICHELLE

Debris was first performed at the Latchmere Theatre in April 2003, with the following cast:

MICHAEL, Daniel Harcourt

MICHELLE, Carolyn Tomkinson

Director, Tessa Walker

Designer, Sophie Charalambous

Lighting, Phil Hewit

This production of *Debris* transferred with the same cast to Battersea Arts Centre on 30 March 2004, as part of the *Time Out* Critics' Choice Season.

Cruxicide

MICHAEL: On my sixteenth birthday my father
erected a fourteen-foot crucifix in our living room,
despite the fact that the living room is only eight
foot tall. He considers smashing a hole through,
but – realising that this would take away from the
dramatic effect – decides that the entire ceiling has
to go, and so sets to work with a Kango hammer
on a cleverly constructed trolley, chunks of
ceiling, dust and carpet from the upstairs flat
falling about his shoulders like rain and dandruff.
He attaches foot-long bars horizontally to the back
of the cross, which are then bolted into the wall,
giving the effect of the structure being
freestanding. It's an impressive sight, which is
perhaps only slightly marred by the badly framed
reproductions of spitfires and puppies behind him,
and the shockingly dirty wallpaper of the flat
above.

The foot-ledge is six foot in the air, and my dad –
fond of his bacon and eggs – is a fat bastard. Yet
somehow he makes it. Once up there he is faced
with the problem of staying on, the foot-ledge
being small and at a forty-five degree angle, but
Daddy, practical as ever, has thought ahead and at
torso level two leather straps await. He buckles

himself in, naked, and he pulls on a plastic tag –
like the American police use – and his left arm is
secured to the beam. Then…Then he pulls on a
lever, and the scaffold, the cleverest part of all this,
slowly wheels into position. He slips his right hand
through a tag on that side of the beam and
somehow manages to give it a pull, though
obviously it is not as secure as the other one.

The scaffold. This construction, this ballet of
cleverly put together levers, pulleys, ropes and
sellotape slowly moves forward on tracks, the way
having been painstakingly cleared of rubble and
splintered furniture beforehand. Once in place it
stops, quivering slightly, but ready for action. Four
wooden tags stick out at the height of my father's
mouth painted blue, red, yellow and green (I later
found that the paint was harmless if ingested – a
touching gesture). These tags have been made
from ice-lolly sticks, and if you look on the bottom
you can still read the jokes. I didn't though.

It's time. My dad, firmly secured to his
masterpiece, cranes his neck and grabs the blue
tag with his teeth. Perhaps this was the moment of
doubt, perhaps this was the moment of fear, but he
jerked that tag back anyway. Levers clicked, ropes
tightened, balls rolled, a frog leapt into a bucket
and the trigger of the nail gun poised over the

palm of his left hand was pulled, slamming a six inch nail through his flesh and into the beam of the cross.

He screams.

Fuck! That hurt, that really hurt! Imagine the shock on my daddy's face as a fix of pain slams into his brain. Flesh rips, the delicate bones of the palm are pushed aside and splintered as a blasphemous intrusion of steel screams through his hand. Imagine him panting, gasping, muttering to himself, sobbing. Imagine him pulling the red tag – you can't? Well he does, he does and his right hand is nailed to the beam.

He screams.

Surely this is enough. Don't you think that this is enough? No Daddy, please, no more, not the yellow tag Pop, please Daddy, you're scaring me – Daddy no! But yes! He pulls it and an extra large nail smashes through the bones of both feet, impaling them to that forty-five degree foot-ledge and making the crucifixion complete. There is silence now apart from the irregular breathing of my Dad and the drip of his blood onto the floor.

After what seems like an age my father pulls himself together and goes for that green tag. He slowly reaches out, grabs it with his teeth, and with what's left of his strength he pulls it back. A pin is loosened, the scaffold wobbles for a second, then falls back with a crump and a dramatic billow of dust.

Pause.

Four hours later the living room door is pushed open and I walk in. No presents, no ice cream, no jelly, no vodka, no spotty teens being misunderstood, no screaming children singing happy birthday, just a pile of rubble, scaffold, and my dad dying on the cross. My sixteenth birthday. My coming of age. I hesitantly pick my way through the disaster area, as my father, slowly surfacing from the agony that has become his world, looks down on me. He is very pale. Almost blue. His glistening white body looks like it is made of dough. At some point the contents of his bowels had sprayed themselves across the back of his legs and the upright of the crucifix. He wheezes and gurgles, his lungs filled with fluid, and snot, sweat and spittle dribble down his fat chops. His penis has been made tiny by adrenaline and pain, and the weight of him seems to have stretched the holes in his feet.

Now my old man is not stupid. Think of what he's constructed, think of what he's achieved, think of his eye for detail – think of the paint. He knows exactly how long it takes to die on the cross. He knows exactly what time I will open the door. I'm not saying it's a cry for help, I'm not saying it's a prank that went wrong, I'm not saying that it was an accusatory gesture, but what I am saying is that when I looked into his eyes they were not the eyes of a suicide.

Looking at me now he musters the last remnants of his strength. This is it, this is the moment, the crowning glory of his achievement: he must find it within himself, he must, he must. His head lifts millimetre by millimetre, his mouth opens, dribble and bile spattering to the ground, and from somewhere within that body comes a voice, a sound, a sentence:

'My son, my son, why have you forsaken me?'

And as these words leave the air his head rolls onto his chest. There. He's done it. It's over. Now he can rest. It's over.

So he thinks. I look at him. Surely this wasn't how Jesus looked? Surely Our Lord had a bit more style, a bit more élan, a bit more pizzazz. He looks utterly disgusting up there on his fourteen-foot crucifix, his head in the home of the another flat, his feet in ours. He thinks it's over. But it's not.

'Forgive me father, for I know not what I do.'

And with that I carefully back away. I'm almost at the door before the meaning of this has got through his pain. I watch it trickle through his brain, and suddenly he looks at me in absolute terror.

Slowly, I leave, closing the door behind me.

The Last Chicken on Earth

MICHELLE: My mother died of Joy. On the day that I was born, while I sat there hanging in my mother's fluid, suspended in aspic, my thumb in my mouth, my mother and father experienced a wave of joy so profound that as it washed over them and frothed on their skins they instinctively knew that not to find expression for this heat would mean the end of all three of us, the fabric of our bodies collapsing on a molecular level in the face of such extremes of energy and so my dad cooked a chicken. He had seen this on TV. A man cooking a chicken. He had to do this because of the bundle of life wrapped up in my mother's belly – me, yes me – a mess of skin, flesh, bone, placenta and god's holy bounty about to become detached and walk amongst them bringing happiness and purpose to their lives. That was how they felt. It was. You can imagine their irritating smiles as they sat in expectant silence, this ever expanding growth of chromosomes rendering words useless, occasionally catching each other's eye and laughing like streams, my dad capering now in the kitchen, if a sixteen stone man who in all probability was pissed can be said to caper.

Chicken was definitely the answer. When this man on the telly cooked chicken you could tell that he understood joy, you could tell that that man there was life, that man there with the chicken, that man that understood joy, that man there on the telly cooking that chicken who understood joy, that man there, that there, that there was life and my dad knew that, which is why he cooked a chicken for my mum, just like that man there on the telly because of joy, and the joy was me, I was the joy, you see, I was the joy. Me. I was their joy.

My dad brings in the chicken in triumph, held high above his head like a cooked chicken held high above his head and deep down on my mother's liver I experience the thrill of expectation that races through her bloodstream, hear the gentle flutter of butterflies wings near my ear, and can't help but feel caught up in this general feeling that things are going to be good, that fortune is smiling, that god is handing out lollies and I grin to myself around my now fully formed thumb and kick playfully at my mother's spleen. They begin to eat the chicken, which is, to be honest, a little dry and overcooked, but they begin to eat the chicken as if it were the last chicken on earth, grinning at each other through the grease on their chins and occasionally tossing a half eaten wing to

my brother who lies in the corner paddling around
in his own excrement, though all fairness he was,
unlike me, a mistake and not wanted and it all sort
of went horribly wrong with him so you can
hardly blame them for wanting to start again, so
maybe you shouldn't think about him, so forget
what I said about him, okay, he's not there.

And then a bone gets caught in my mother's throat
and she begins to die. A little cough and they
giggle at this teasing burp, shovelling more
chicken down their gullets, my father swallowing,
my mother dying. A halting wheeze and again
they giggle though my mother betrays an ounce of
uncertainty as she winkles flesh from a tiny rib
with her left incisor. And then she's waving,
choking, pointing at her back and clutching her
throat, still clinging to her chicken but unable to
breath. My dad, still consumed with joy, gambols
around behind her and gives her a playful tap on
the neck, but seeing her lips turn blue begins to
panic, to roar, to scream, punches her in the back
of the head, desperate to dislodge the obstruction,
while I, caught up in the panic, push my groping
arm pointlessly upwards, dad smacking her in the
back of the head with his shovel, bellowing at god,
my child, my child, my wife and my child.

My mother now staggers around the room like a dying dinosaur about to fall on a car and suddenly in a flash of inspiration my dad remembers the Heimlich manoeuvre and grabs my mother around the waist, his fists clamping around my neck like a meat scarf, tensing, ready, flexing, about to…

'NO!'

Coughs my mother with the last wisps of her breath and wrenches herself from his grasp spinning around to face him, her hands wrapped protectively on what she thought was my head but was in fact her pancreas. They stare at each other, knowing. Realising. My father almost blind with panic, my mother calming him with her gaze as her life bleeds away, somehow making him understand that they had to choose, me or her, and they chose me, you see, they chose me, through the pain and the anguish and the tears and despair they chose me, and my mother died there in my father's arms as his soul exploded and the TV found itself crashing through the window and smashing into the concrete four floors below.

And they chose me.

It was very touching.

It was.

Very.

Very touching.

It was.

Divorce

MICHAEL: This boy…this boy in this pizza place I was looking at through this window, I was looking at this boy through this window, staring at this boy who sat opposite this man in a suit, the only communication the boy flicking his olives onto the man's pizza, the man eating them, the man spitting the stones into the palm of his hand, the hand placing them in the metal ashtray with a soft click where they sat like wide eyed children watching this silent production line, waiting for their parents to speak, I had seen…this before. Where? Where had I seen this before? I stayed and watched. I followed, I followed them, when they left I followed them but at a discreet distance through many twisting streets, past shops and then hedges, trees, low walls and doors that were all different from each other. They went into the house, up to, they went up to the house, up to the, the man pushed the buzzer the boy got out a key, and the door opened before the key was…before he could…with the key, he… It was a woman, of course, she hugged the boy who went inside and they talked, the man and woman, irritated, I think she was a little irritated but they kissed goodbye like aunts and the man went away, where had I seen this before? I stayed. I watched. I looked in

through the windows. I saw the boy watching TV.
I saw the mother talking, talking on the phone. I
saw a glass of wine. I saw cooked vegetables. I
saw her hair. I saw homework. I saw pyjamas. I
saw him talking, talking on the phone. I saw him
talking to her. I saw. I saw. And

I

Saw

Him

Lying

In her

Lap.

I had seen this before. Through windows of TV
shops I had seen this on TVs through the windows
of TV shops before, I had seen this before, this
was how people, perhaps this was how people
lived.

Pause.

I broke in through a very small toilet window,
quite high up, but not so high that I couldn't reach,
the atmosphere immediately different, the smell of
other people, the sound of the TV, the warmth of
the air all crowding around and brushing my skin
like her hair. I crept gently and quietly forward

into the living room and crouched between the door and the couch, her and her boy sitting there, his head in her lap, her hands stroking his head and them watching TV. I listened to their talk. I smelled her shampoos and soaps. I watched telly inches away from them, sitting there crouched at the end of their sofa, listening to their talk and purrs and all three of us were happy, oh yes, we were, we were all three happy.

Pause.

The scream ripped through my flesh like a nail fired from a gun, imbedding itself in the delicate bones of my inner ear so that if I concentrate I can still hear it there now. For one tiny endless eggshell second we all three hovered there facing each other, not wanting to move in case the moment shattered like glass. Then she hurled her son, the boy, through the door, the kitchen, the kitchen door which leads to the kitchen, where there was a phone, in the kitchen there was a phone and she pushed her son through that door, following herself, while I ran for the other one, the one at the front of the house the front door. I belted away into the night, the scream hurting, water blinding, snot choking, ran, I ran, I ran fast and hard away and there was a siren, behind me, a siren was behind me fast, I ran fast, the scream

there in my ear in in my heart, I ran and looked
left, right, somewhere to hide from the scream
behind me, so I turned into flats, an estate, though
the car was still behind, in the estate, I was
running on an estate – or in an estate – running,
turning, the siren / scream with me everywhere,
one turn a door open I jumped in, into smell, just
bad smell a where people throw their, down a
chute into a where people chuck their thrown
away into a pile rubbish, a pile of rubbish, in the in
the in the in the in the, a pile of rubbish, in the in
the in the in the in the, a pile of rubbish, in the.

Pause.

About half an hour later I heard a rustle beside
me.

Unclearry

MICHAEL is strangling MICHELLE, who is kneeling on the floor, her face turning red, then purple, then blue. It is taking a huge amount of effort and goes on for some time. Slowly he looks up and still trying with all his might to crush his sister's neck, he speaks through clenched teeth.

MICHAEL: Killing my sister was proving almost impossible, due to the tenacity with which she clung to her life.

Suddenly he lets go of her, exhausted. She collapses on the floor, gasping, coughing and rubbing her neck. He puts his hands into his armpits as if they were burnt. There is a long silence. MICHAEL shakes his hands and blows on them, and then puts them under his arms again.

Fuck!

MICHELLE: (*Her voice a croak.*) You swore.

MICHAEL: What?

MICHELLE: You shouldn't swear.

MICHAEL: Sorry.

Long pause.

My hands hurt.

MICHELLE slowly climbs to her feet, unsteady and coughing. She crosses over to her brother, takes his hands in hers and begins to rub them. He winces.

MICHELLE: Don't be such a baby.

Shamed, he allows her to rub the life back into his hands. He feels better.

It's your own fault.

MICHAEL: I have to kill you.

MICHELLE: No you don't.

MICHAEL: I do!

MICHELLE: Who said?

MICHAEL: He won't take both of us.

MICHELLE: (*To the audience.*) That's not true.

(*To MICHAEL.*) That's not true.

MICHAEL: (*To MICHELLE.*) It is!

(*To the audience.*) It is!

MICHELLE: You see the problem was that I'd got a little upset when Unclearry –

MICHAEL: Who isn't really our uncle.

MICHELLE: Better that an uncle.

MICHAEL: Much better.

MICHELLE: – had stolen us.

MICHAEL: Rescued us.

MICHELLE: Alright, rescued us. But that's only natural.

MICHAEL: You wanna go back?

MICHELLE: Fuck off!

They are both shocked. Pause.

MICHAEL: You blubbed like a baby.

MICHELLE: I was cold. I was scared. We'd been sitting outside the Crown and Goose for fourteen hours with no more to sustain us than a lemonade each and a pack of monster munch.

MICHAEL: At last Dad came out.

MICHELLE: His arm 'round Unclearry.

MICHAEL: Vomit down his shirt making him look like he'd had his throat cut.

MICHELLE: Dad's conversion to Catholicism had been hotly followed by the customary Jesus fixation, and now he drank nothing but water and wine.

MICHAEL: Though mostly wine.

MICHELLE: They both looked at us and Unclearry says:

MICHAEL: Those yours?

MICHELLE: In reply, Daddy, never a man of many words, farted loudly and fell flat on his face.

MICHAEL: You're a lucky man, my friend.

MICHELLE: Said Unclearry, but by this time Daddy was already in the land of nod.

'Ow old are ya?

MICHAEL: Twelve, I said.

MICHELLE: Nine and three quarters.

MICHAEL: Said my sister, squeezing out every month she could get. He looked at us long and hard.

MICHELLE: What lovely ages you 'ave.

MICHAEL: And suddenly, Unclearry –

MICHELLE: Not before taking Dad's wallet.

MICHAEL: For petrol he said.

MICHELLE: – grabbed us both, stuck us in his car, and sped off into the cold December night.

MICHAEL: And that's when you started blubbing.

MICHELLE: Which prompted Unclearry to nudge him in the ribs and through a cloud of Johnnywalkerfaggarlicgas utter:

MICHAEL: Girls, eh? What can we do with 'em?

MICHELLE: But that don't mean you should kill me!

MICHAEL: What else can I do? You wanna go back to the Crown and Goose?

MICHELLE: But what about Mister Bought and Smite?

MICHAEL: He won't take you.

MICHELLE: That's not fair!

MICHAEL: I'm sorry.

MICHELLE: I want to live with Mister Bought and Smite as well! I want to live in a big house with ice cream and servants and champagne.

MICHAEL: You don't even know what champagne is.

She sits down to sulk. During this speech MICHAEL crosses to get a cup and then brings it back to his sister.

And so she went on. But what she couldn't see was the look that Unclearry had given me when we was in the car, when he had said that about girls.

Though hideously ugly in his stained tweed jacket and diamond cut jumper, though drooling and smelling of piss, I could tell he was a kind man – he had to be, otherwise why rescue us from our lives. That look on a more lowly human being might have been mistaken for greed, for avarice, for lascivious hunger, for vulturious lust, but on that kind and saintly man I knew he was worried that his good deed would come a cropper because she was a Girl.

He hands the cup to MICHELLE who is rubbing her throat.

MICHELLE: Ta.

She takes a gulp and immediately spits it out. She starts coughing and gasping.

MICHAEL: Drink it: it's good for you.

MICHELLE: What is it?

MICHAEL: Bleach.

MICHELLE: Bleach?

MICHAEL: Yeah. It'll kill ya.

MICHELLE: (*Throwing the cup down.*) I don't wanna be killed!

Long pause.

And so we waited. I was sure he was wrong, otherwise why would Unclearry take me as well? Why not leave me there with my Daddy, waiting for the sun to rise over the Crown and Goose like a hangover? Mister Bought and Smite would want a boy and a girl, the poor lonely man.

MICHAEL: I don't wanna go back.

MICHELLE: Me neither.

MICHAEL: This is a dream come true. Like getting something you actually want for Christmas.

MICHELLE: I used to dream of being abducted by aliens.

MICHAEL: Of contracting a rare and highly contagious disease.

MICHELLE: Of being adopted.

MICHAEL: Or of being taken into care.

Pause.

Anyone arks ya...

MICHELLE: Says Unclearry.

MICHAEL: An' I'm your Unclearry.

MICHELLE: Which is stupid coz that's who he was.

MICHAEL: And do as I fucking well tell ya!

MICHELLE: Unclearry's tone had changed as he got out of the car and headed towards a derelict slum.

MICHAEL: Must be the pressure. Poor man.

MICHELLE: And then he locked us in a room.

MICHAEL: I gots calls to make.

MICHELLE: And with that he was off. And so we waited.

Pause. They wait.

Unclearry bursts in, breathless and excited and smelling like a drunken cabbage, his lips curl back and expose his rotten teeth and at first we flinch but then it slowly dawns on us. He's smiling.

MICHAEL: Good news, good and beautiful news! He's here. The man we've been waiting for, Mr fucking wonderful himself! Now I want you to be good little angels and smile as pretty as you can – cause if you don't…!

(*He smiles again.*) Remember the big house. Remember the ice cream. Remember the servants and champagne. But most of all remember the back of my fucking hand! And if you start blubbing…

(*As himself.*) I knew I should've killed her.

...there'll be hell to pay. Now kiddies, think of nice things and put your hands together for the marvellous, for the fabulous, for the sophisticated, for the stinking fucking rich...

MICHELLE / MICHAEL: (*Together, in wonder as he enters.*) Mister Bought and Smite!

Debris

MICHAEL: I used to believe that babies were found under gooseberry bushes. I had heard that they were delivered by storks, dropped gently down chimneys to land in little white bundles of fluff. I even once believed that we were brought into this world by the miracle of conception, gestation and then childbirth, but I now know that not to be the case. Like mushrooms, babies grow in rubbish. They construct themselves from rotting leaves, coke cans, syringes and empty packets of monster munch and wait for their parents to find them. I know this to be the truth. Because I found one.

Beside me this rustling sound, rustling beside me, in the dark, smell, rustling in, I was still sweating, hiding and beside me there was this rustling in, in the dark and I look down in a shaft from the street light, from the crack in the door I had to push open the door to let in a shaft of street light in a crack so I could see, which cut across the rubbish and illuminated a, a hand, a very small hand. A very small hand. A very small baby. It was a very small baby in the rubbish.

I reach down, my hand, reach with my hand and push aside washing powder boxes and ladies tights and pull out a very small baby, greens clinging to its head browns covering its hand and I pull out a very small baby and lift it up a very small naked cold baby, a boy a little boy, and I pull out a very small cold naked baby boy, my boy, my boy I pull out my boy. What happened inside was an organ in my chest dissolved, was teleported from me, into me, out of me, turned to snow, into warmth into golden blood which rushed through my veins and turned my mind into fire, my body into blazing scream, laugh, I didn't know what was – instinct kicked in, inside, instinct burned around my body like adrenaline, like gin, burned around my body destroying my mind in a second, in a flash, searing the shadow of it against the inside of my skull and replacing it with something else, something new, something very different, a new, a new…

He was very cold. Dying. He was dying. I sat there for an hour, I was there for an hour sat in other people's rubbish with a dying baby in my arms rocking back and forth and I was happy, oh yes, I was happy. I look down, his lips are like – ebbing, his life is – slugs, his lips like tiny grey slugs – fading, his lips moving slightly, little circles made from his hands in the air surrounding us, floating around us, tiny ice cubes, he was cold so with my shirt, I opened my shirt because panic

was now pushing its way through, I was beginning
to panic because to find and then lose, so I opened
my shirt I hid him close to me, I wrapped him in
me I dragged him into me into my love, rocking,
close to my heart, the circles becoming smaller
now as he became weaker, though warmth began,
it was maybe too late, I could see his slugs lips, in
his lips, weakness, hunger draining his cold,
draining into me, his life draining out of him, his
movements going, leaving him and I pulled him
to me and rocked faster because what else could I
do?

And somehow

He finds his way to my breast.

*He screams as the baby bites into him. He gasps with
pain and anguish, still holding the child, writhing but
not wanting to disturb it. He begins to get used to it as
he looks down at the baby.*

And he fed at my breast. Not milk but blood. He
slowly drinks what life he can from my tiny
nipple, his grey lips becoming red, his hand
waving, and I feel that surge of feeling burst
through my chest again, flooding my body, my
mind. It's love. Isn't it. It's love. I look down at
my boy, my son, my...my...feeding there,
my...my...life pounding back into him,

my…my…Rubbish? Garbage? Debris. Good name. Sounds French. Be able to get him into posh schools with a name like that. My Debris. My Debris.

Necroviviparity

MICHELLE: No…

My Mother died of an observation. The observation was not hers. She rejected death by overdose, by murder, by gas explosion, by unsuccessful surgery, by diphtheria, by typhoid, by stabbing and by old age to die of ennui. Whilst watching a late night arts program – not her customary fare – and eating a jar of pickled onions – her customary fare – she happened to hear one of the panel remark:

'Of course, it's impossible to create anything original these days.'

She stops mid-chew, another onion halfway to her mouth, puts her other hand on her balloon of a stomach, and lets the ramifications sink in. But she's creating something new, isn't she? Something original in her belly? That moving kicking wrapped-up ball of six months flesh, surely that's original? But she knows. It is not so much the certainty of the remark itself but the nodding way in which the rest of those intellectuals and artists greet it, as if it was understood by everyone in the world. Except my mother.

Her face slowly slackens, the jaw loosening, the cheeks hollowing, the muscles in the eyes becoming soft as kidney. Her arm drops and the pickled onion falls, bouncing once, twice, then rolling to the TV as if taking sides, the little round bastard.

She stares.

For a long time.

The picture on the screen fades into a little dot, turns to fuzz, and then the next morning, bursts into life again and still my mother stares. And, as that night the picture fades again into a pickled onion, so my mum, relinquishing her life, fades into a corpse, leaving that poor defenceless child in her belly – namely me – to fend for herself.

After a brief period of mourning my father pushes my mommy off the couch and onto the floor and switches over to the football. And there I gestate, in my mother's rotting corpse, protected by her womb, three months of my development yet to go, though I take four seeing as how I'd have to go through the birth unaided. This was the most difficult period, as well you might imagine, defying the laws of life and death so that I may one day take my unoriginal place in that unoriginal world. The womb holds up well but toward the end begins to give way to the bacteria so that it has to be patched up with other parts of my mother's anatomy, such as the spleen or a handful of liver, not to mention the odd empty crisp packet that my groping hand finds lying on the floor.

On the first of May I burst forth from between my mother's legs to make my pigheaded and painstaking way towards her breast, but find there a source of sustenance only a plant could find a use for. And so I push my mouth onto that mound of stagnant jelly and allow my lips to take root, my tongue to turn tuber, so as to partake of the goodness that is my birthright. Over the coming months I sprout leaves – which of course I have subsequently shed – that cleverly turn towards the sun, the better to aid photosynthesis, my mouth and nose being already fully employed and me with a desperate need for oxygen. And all that time I eye up the TV. Coz I know. Coz I haven't forgotten. Coz I remember.

Poor Mummy. She had forgotten that the little men are not real, that it's just a magic box, that words are no more than an ever increasingly abstract collection if sounds in the air. The reality was in her belly, the reality was growing inside, the reality was me – plant child sucking death through a potato tongue – that was reality.

I throw out tendrils everywhere to gain more life, my father of course – not being the most affectionate of men – brushes them aside, but mostly I push them towards that glowing box in the corner, towards my foe. It is a painstaking process, taking almost a year, but I get there in the end. Little is left of my mother by this stage, just a few dirty bones and some brown sludge, but the pickled onion is doing surprisingly well soaked as it is in it's spicy malt vinegar and hidden from my fat dad by the leg of the telly. Now I crawl to that box, my tendrils slowly closing like a fist I am a snake a boa constrictor a hand a fist around an egg squeezing poised to crush... Suddenly there is a movement behind me. It's daddy. He has noticed what is going on, not-televisual sight at this desperate moment finally penetrating his meat-head.

'NO!'

He Screams.

I stop.

I look round at him.

There is only pain in his face.

Infinite loss. A voice barely audible.

'Not the telly!'

Pause. She reconsiders.

Squeeze.

She screams and falls to the floor.

(*Raising her head.*) He gets up. He looks around. He is like a man possessed released of his demons, blinking in the sunlight. He sees our mum. He sees our dead mum.

Something in my father snapped that day.

Telly

MICHAEL: So in the dark, out of that rubbish tip, smell, I left, went home, made my way home with, went home with Debris, with my boy, with my boy Debris and my new mind, through the streets but I see nothing, around me there was nothing, nothing around me just a burn held close to my chest, melting, this boy melting the rocks inside, a small tiny cold fire held close to my chest, though not so cold now, not so, not so, not so cold now, the lips, full red lips now, and maybe a smile, I'm not sure, maybe a smile, the smile even the hint of which was enough to stand my hair on end with tiny crackles of blue lightning tracing a path up each fibre to flick and disappear with a seismic tingle through my bones, this was my boy, this was my boy, this was my Debris.

At four in the morning I would crawl from my bed and sleepwalk to the cardboard box where I kept him, to be jolted awake by a stab of pure agony receding into pure love. I bounced him on my knee, and when I burped him little red traces of myself would trickle from his mouth onto my shoulder and a tiny cloud that tasted like guinness would drift into my face. And we were happy. Oh yes. We were happy.

My sister. My sister, I let my sister in on, I had to, I had to let my sister in on this secret, because she would've, she definitely would've found out, and I needed, I needed some help, hiding, hiding him from my dad, and she would help, watching, I felt her watching the boy with me and I felt something else, from her, coming from her, emanating, this feeling of, I couldn't quite make it out as she watched us, but she kept watch and I was able, became able, was able to look after the boy while she watched, and planted an idea in my head.

MICHELLE: You gonna grow him up here?

MICHAEL: Yeah.

MICHELLE: Here?

MICHAEL: Yeah.

MICHELLE: Here?

MICHAEL: Yeah.

MICHELLE: You gonna grow him up here?

MICHAEL: Yes.

Pause.

MICHELLE: We ain't got a telly.

MICHAEL: So?

MICHELLE: They need a telly.

MICHAEL: This was true.

They do. They do need a telly. I looked at us. I looked at the world outside. I looked at him. How could he be like them? How could he move through them? My blood wasn't enough. I left him with my sister while I went out looking for a telly.

Mister Bought and Smite

MICHELLE: (*As Mister Bought and Smite.*) Why what a fabulously charming place you have: how novel to allow your brown floral wallpaper to peel from the brickwork, how clever of you to have covered every conceivable surface with dirt. It's simply so earthy, so bohemian, so wanton, so ...*pauvre.* Jeremy Boughton-Smythe at your service, or rather you at mine, you must be Arry.

MICHAEL: ...

MICHELLE: To have broken this chair to splinters, to have cracked this decaying plaster, to have smashed all the windows, to have infected this carpet with fleas shows a delicate eye for detail that one cannot help but admire. I'm convinced we shall be firm friends. Is this faecal matter human or animal?

MICHAEL: ...

MICHELLE: Ignore me! Forgive my craven display of shallility. When gazing upon the Mona Lisa one does not enquire where Da Vinci brought his paint. You are a rare genius, Arry. I shall compose a poem in your honour at once.

MICHAEL: ...

MICHELLE: And this is Guy…

MICHAEL walks forward as Guy.

My gorilla.

(*As herself.*) And the room shrank to the size of a matchbox as the biggest man in the world walked through that door.

MICHAEL: Our mouths dropped.

MICHELLE: Yes I know, he is a trifle crude but you must admit, terribly effective. And he plays the harpsichord like an angel. Now, Arry…

MICHAEL: Sir.

MICHELLE: I believe you have something for me. Or rather some things.

MICHAEL: And Unclearry pushed us toward Mister Bought and Smite.

MICHELLE: Never had we seen anything like it.

MICHAEL: Mister Bought and Smite so clean and crisp that it was painful to look at him.

MICHELLE: And the biggest cruellest man in the world at his shoulder, with eyes that showed he had no thoughts in his tiny brain that were not directed towards his nose, which he was now industriously picking.

(*As Mister Bought and Smite.*) Ah children,
children...

MICHAEL: Said Mister Bought and Smite.

MICHELLE: What delightful specimens you are.

MICHAEL: And he pulled out two lollies.

MICHELLE: One for you, my precious young
Ganymede...

MICHAEL: Which greedily I took.

MICHELLE: And one for you my delicious little
nymphet.

(*As herself.*) Teacher said I shouldn't take sweets off
strang...

MICHAEL: (*As Unclearry.*) Take it you little shit!

MICHELLE: Said Unclearry, slapping the back of
my head. But no sooner had I said 'ow' than
Mister Bought and Smite clicked his fingers and
his gorilla lazily unfolded one huge arm, the fist of
which connected with Unclearry's head and sent
him flying into an already demolished couch,
while the index finger of his other hand pulled out
a bogey the size of a baby's head. This he ate.

Arry you scamp. Forgive him children: he is
merely high-spirited. Now. Down to business.
Would you like to come with Mr Boughton-

Smythe, off to his hise in the country and there to
be treated like royalty for the rest of your youths,
or would you like to go back to your dingy little
council flat to face a life of chips and petty crime?
Take your time, no hurry, but tell me now. Do you
want to come with me?

Pause.

MICHAEL: He was a stranger.

MICHELLE: He had a gorilla.

MICHAEL: Who had smacked Unclearry clear
across the room.

MICHELLE: But he had a big house.

MICHAEL: And such big words.

MICHELLE: And he smelt so…nice!

Pause.

MICHELLE / MICHAEL: (*Together.*) Yes!

MICHELLE: (*As Mister Bought and Smite.*) Ah, and so
it is settled. Arry?

MICHAEL: Who was extracting himself from the
remains of the couch.

MICHELLE: Have them delivered to me this
afternoon. Guy?

MICHAEL steps forward as Guy.

Show Mr Arry how you peel a banana.

He mimes peeling a banana and throwing away the skin.

Show Mr Arry what you do to people who disappoint me?

He does the same mime.

A bargain has been struck, Arry. Do not disappoint me. And with this I take my leave. On Thursday I am dining with Lady Toynbee – do you know her? Of the Shropshire Toynbees – and you simply must come along. But do bathe first. One can take irony only so far.

MICHAEL: And with that he was gone. Unclearry waited for a minute, then leapt into the air and danced around the room rubbing his hands and screamed with laughter.

(*As Unclearry.*) Yes! Yesyesyesyesyes!

(*As himself.*) Unclearry was happy.

MICHELLE: It was good to see Unclearry happy. And then he turned to us.

MICHAEL: Well my little darlings…

MICHELLE: Said Unclearry.

MICHAEL: ...you've behaved yourself very well. Very well indeed! Unclearry is pleased, and you're going off to live in the big house.

MICHELLE: Hooray!

MICHAEL: But first...

MICHELLE: Said Unclearry.

MICHAEL: ...to show you how pleased I am...

MICHELLE: And he began to move towards us...

MICHAEL: ...we're going to play a little game...

MICHELLE: ...a strange expression on his face.

MICHAEL: ...a little game of...

MICHELLE: We like games.

MICHAEL: ...affection.

MICHELLE: This confused us.

MICHAEL: You may as well get used to it now...

MICHELLE: And slowly, Unclearry reached out his hands to us...

Suddenly the door bursts open...

MICHAEL: Smashing my sister in the face, of course.

MICHELLE: ...and there in the doorway...

MICHAEL: Angry as thunder…

MICHELLE: Bigger than ever before…

MICHAEL: Vomit still clinging to his ears…

MICHELLE: Dad!

MICHAEL: Shhh! Unclearry drops us as quick as a flash, and begins to back away like a frightened rabbit.

MICHELLE: But before he can bolt our bull of a father – who hasn't yet seen us – steams forward and pins him by his throat to the wall!

MICHAEL: Good ta see ya!

MICHELLE: Squeaks Unclearry.

MICHAEL: I can explain everything.

MICHELLE: You fhacking bastard!

MICHAEL: Bellows Daddy.

MICHELLE: I'll Fhacking 'ave you!

MICHAEL: And pulls back his fist to pound that face into the wall. Unclearry thinks quicker than he's ever done before, and whips out Dad's wallet.

(*As Unclearry.*) Here y'are!

MICHELLE: Says Unclearry.

MICHAEL: No harm done.

MICHELLE: Father, with one hand still to Unclearry's throat, takes the wallet, opens it up and checks the contents. And there we see a little red blinking light.

MICHAEL: Being a careful man – some would say a tight bastard – our father had had his wallet fitted with a tracking device.

MICHELLE: A thoughtful precaution that he somehow never felt necessary to bestow upon his children. He pockets the wallet and looks deep into Unclearry's eyes.

My kids. I want my kids.

MICHAEL: Ah, now leave me the kiddies, eh?

MICHELLE: I want my kids.

MICHAEL: I can pay.

MICHELLE: I want my kids.

MICHAEL: More money than you can drink in a year!

MICHELLE: I want my fhacking kids!

MICHAEL: And can it be?

MICHELLE: We see him there.

MICHAEL: The same dad he's always been.

MICHELLE: Smelly and drunk.

MICHAEL: Angry and thick.

MICHELLE: Big and stupid.

MICHAEL: But there is a tear in his eye.

MICHELLE: And he is willing – and I swear it's true – to squeeze the life out of another mans neck to get his children back.

They exchange a look. She makes a decision.

Dad!!

MICHAEL: Shhhh!

MICHELLE: Daddy, Daddy!!!

MICHAEL: Shut up!

MICHELLE: Dad, Daddy, Daddy, DAD!

Pause.

MICHAEL: And Daddy turns 'round and at last notices us – Unclearry sliding to the floor unseen in his own private world of fear – and the tear that was in his eye rolls down his cheek, over his vomit encrusted lips, and hits the floor with a sound like the worlds biggest heartbeat. He looks down at us. He says:

MICHELLE: Every man has his crosses to bear.

MICHAEL: And he turns sadly and heads for the door. He stops there. He seems to be quivering. And over his shoulder he says:

MICHELLE: Come on you little cunts!

MICHAEL: And we follow him out.

MICHELLE: Thinking sadly of peeled bananas.

MICHAEL: Of Ice cream and servants.

MICHELLE: Of something called champagne.

MICHAEL: And I know that my tenacious little sister is thinking…

MICHELLE: That you should've squeezed just a little bit harder.

I look at my brother

And something in him has changed.

Something is different.

An awareness.

He is now aware

That there are lives different from ours.

Things won't be the same.

In the Beginning

MICHAEL: ...dragging home this, in my hands, it's heavy, this TV is heavy, I'm dragging home this TV, my mind is light, racing, like an engine out of gear, spinning through, and in my hands this thing is, this thing is heavy, I can feel my breast heavy, pulsing with blood, aching with blood and my mind beats with thoughts one after the other, one thought kicking the other out, throwing the, forcing the, but soon it's one, just one, just one thought endlessly replacing itself endlessly as I carry, as I drag, as I heave, one thought, the thought of my boy, the only thought, no longer thinking of my dad's, to the telly, his reaction to what I'm, not of my sister hiding Debris just for those hours, not of the feeling which emanating from, the feeling which I hadn't, but just one relentless thought, my boy, my boy, my boy, my boy, my boy, my boy, my boy, my boy, my boy, my boy Debris, that's the only thought, so when I, I go in, when I go in and see, look at, see the face on my sister, her face has this look and my heart drains of blood, ice, my body walks into a soft concrete wall, her face, her look is an expletive from God, a cup of bleach in the eyes, a full stop, a sound too loud to hear, so I know something is, I instantly know something is not, I know in that instant that something is not right. And she is not holding my boy. She is not holding Debris. I follow her eyes. My dad sits on the couch cradling Debris in his arms. My father and my son. And her.

MICHELLE: He came in.

MICHAEL: Panic pounding, breath catching, eyes stinging what the what the what the what the what the –

MICHELLE: He came in.

MICHAEL: What?

MICHELLE: I was just playing with the boy and he came in, he just came in.

MICHAEL: Why didn't you lock the –

MICHELLE: I forgot. I must've forgot. I…He hasn't hurt it. He…it's weird.

MICHAEL: – holding my boy, sitting there, he was just sitting, he was just sitting there holding my boy and the look, my sister's face had this look, and I knew, I knew that she had done this – on purpose, I knew that she had done this on purpose…

MICHELLE: He just came in.

MICHAEL: You've done this on purpose.

MICHELLE: He hasn't hurt it.

MICHAEL: – holding my, holding my, holding
my –

MICHELLE: It's weird. Look.

MICHAEL: I looked. And then…

MICHELLE: …the strangest…

MICHAEL: …thing…

MICHELLE: …that we had…

MICHAEL: …ever, in our…

MICHELLE: …lives seen…

MICHAEL: …happened. He began to talk to
the baby.

MICHELLE: You are so beautiful. Your fingers.
Your perfect little fingers. Your little nails.

MICHAEL: He didn't shout. He didn't growl. He
didn't scream. He didn't snarl. He talked. We'd
never seen him do that. We were transfixed.

MICHELLE: So beautiful. (*To someone who isn't there.*)
Beautiful. You've made such a beautiful boy.

He began to talk to someone who wasn't there.

MICHAEL: – holding my, holding my, holding my
and my soul freezes, it screams, it becomes solid

57

mercury and shatters into a thousand tiny sharp pieces and the pieces are the only things I my mind, screaming pain into my brain –

MICHELLE: He had to be beautiful, coz you are.

He's talking to my mother.

MICHAEL: – My brain is full of them –

MICHELLE: – like a crown of thorns –

This is where our lives begin.

MICHAEL: So I go to the phone, the phone, remember? The phone, another phone another house a normal house, but this is a different phone, a phone in the street –

MICHELLE: The hope, the possibility.

MICHAEL: – and I call I call the people who would take because this I cannot have this I cannot watch, this joy, this hope, this hope, this possibility for another I call the people

MICHELLE: My father and my mother.

MICHAEL: – I call the people –

MICHELLE: In the beginning.

MICHAEL: I call the people who would take my I call the people who would take my boy away.

Long pause.

MICHELLE: In the beginning

There is god,

And he's bored.

He's bored shitless.

He wanders around for an eternity of eternities,

Scratching his balls,

Fuck all to do.

So:

Ten billion years ago he makes a bang

And he waits.

Six billion years and the gases and dirt squish together to form the earth,

And he waits, watching, as a billion years later

Primitive single cell organisms with no nuclei form in a piece of mucus.

Within three hundred million years there are animals and plants in the oceans,

God watching in anticipation as in another couple of hundred million years

The plants develop the courage to try their luck on dry land,

Followed by hungry animals that are scared of being lonely.

He watches happily as sixty five million years ago an asteroid smashes into the earth,

And the dinosaurs realise they're too big and stupid to survive,

And it's around this time that a little thing that looks like a lemur makes it's appearance.

Twelve million years ago the lemurs' descendants part company with their friends,

One branch becoming orang-utans, one becoming us,

And time now whizzes past as primates become human,

As they pick up rocks and smash each other over the head,

As they domesticate plants, push out the Neanderthals, learn language and become aware that something is watching.

Wars come and go, slavery, cannibalism, persecution, torture, the invention of the wheel, the invention of the factory,

And eventually this squabbling mass of bipedal fury finally coalesces into my mother and father,

And now god is watching, he's on the edge of his fucking seat, dribbling in anticipation.

He watches their love, their marriage, their fights, their arguments, their first born, the conception and gestation of a little girl, and there we are and there god is on, on that day, that day when my mother complains of pains, terrible pains, and my father, who now knows his life has been denied, my father who sits stunned and drunk in front of the telly watching the life he wants while steeping in the one he hates, ignores her, shouts at her, tells her to fuck herself, she's not due yet, she's got months, it's just wind you fat cunt, and this is the moment, this is the moment and God watches happily as my father refuses, will not, cannot get help, will not believe there's anything –

And suddenly

Her appendix pops.

And she dies.

That was the moment.

That was it.

God sits back.

He rolls a fag.

He grins the satisfaction of a job well done.

He doesn't watch as I am ripped from my mother's corpse on a hospital slab.

He takes little interest in my father's howls.

He doesn't notice my brother scrabbling around alone.

But we know.

We know.

We know that from that moment on God is no longer watching.

Pause.

When they came to take Debris away my father had to be tranquillised with a feather dart before the boy could once more be pried free.

MICHAEL: They found him hiding in someone's garden, a blood red kiss on his cheek from little Debris leaving them in no doubt as to who he was. They say that just before he went under for a second he became absolutely lucid and seemed to be saying sorry to someone who wasn't there.

MICHELLE: When my dad came around he said nothing. He'd given up speaking. But I saw his betrayed eyes following my brother around the flat and hatching a plan to make him see. And we knew –

MICHAEL: – that nothing would be safe from our father's anger.

Every now and then my breast aches and I think of Debris. It's heavy with blood, aching for his lips. And sometimes I fantasize that Babies are not found in rubbish and that somewhere he has a mother whose breast, heavy with milk, throbs in time with mine. I imagine her scared, not of Debris' death, but of his life, placing her boy gently in some warm garbage, unable to cope. I imagine her face. I imagine her tears. I imagine her tears mingling with mine.

MICHELLE / MICHAEL: (*Together.*) I.

Imagine.

Her.

End

LATCHMERE THEATRE

Opened as part of the Gate Theatre in 1982 and re-launched in 2002 as a theatre dedicated to new writing and the new generation of emerging playwrights, the Latchmere Theatre has quickly established itself as one of the most dynamic and exciting new writing venues in London.

> *'The tiny Latchmere Theatre...is carrying the torch for new writing and developing an enviable reputation for spotting the potential of playwrights at the start of their careers.'*
> The Guardian, *November 2003*

Since 2002 the Latchmere Theatre has staged over twenty new plays by important new writers including Phil Porter, Ursula Rani Sarma, Jennifer Farmer, Ronan O'Donnell, Samantha Ellis, Glyn Cannon, Peter Morris, Trevor Williams, Said Sayrafiezadeh, Falk Richter, Anna Marie Murphy as well as new plays by more established playwrights such as Ron Hutchinson, Naomi Wallace and Fraser Grace.

> *'The Latchmere...consistently unearthing some of London theatre's most exciting new voices.'*
> Time Out, *April 2003*

Artistic Director	Paul Higgins
Associate Directors	Johnnie Lyne-Pirkis
	Phil Hewitt
Literary Associate	Matthew Morrison
Artistic Associate	Jennifer MacDonald

Nominated for The Empty Space Peter Brook Theatre Award 2003

Plays premiered at the Latchmere Theatre and published by Oberon Books include *Touched... / Blue* by Ursula Rani Sarma and *Stealing Sweets and Punching People* by Phil Porter. All Oberon Books are available from **www.oberonbooks.com**.